Swoop!

Story by Kathryn Sutherland   Illustrations by Sharyn Madder

Alex liked walking
across the park
on her way to school.
Sometimes her dad went with her
and sometimes her mom
went with her.

One day,
as Dad and Alex were walking along,
something swooped down at them...

S W O O P !

"Dad!" cried Alex. "What was that?"

"That was a magpie!" said Dad.
"Are you hurt?"

"No," said Alex. "But it scared me.
Why did it do that?"

"The magpie must have
a nest near here," said Dad.
"It was trying to scare us away."

4

The next morning, Alex stopped
when they got to the park.
"I don't want the magpie
to swoop down on me again," she said.

"We will go the long way around today,"
said Dad.

But that morning,
Alex was late for school
and Dad was late for work.

When she got home in the afternoon,
Alex said to Mom,
"I don't want that magpie
to swoop at me tomorrow."

"Let's play a trick on it," said Mom.
"I will show you what to do.
Run and get your bike helmet."

"But my bike helmet
won't scare the magpie away,"
said Alex, as she came back with it.

"We will make it look scary!"
said Mom.
"Then the magpie
will stay away from you."

10

"How are we going to do that?"
asked Alex.

"Paint some **very big** eyes,
right in the middle of this cardboard,"
said Mom.

Alex painted the eyes carefully.

Alex and Mom put the cardboard
around the helmet.
Then Alex put it on.
"I look like a monster with big eyes
on top of my head," she said.
"Now I can trick the magpie."

"It will be scared of **you**, now,"
laughed Mom.

The next morning,
Alex felt very brave
as she walked across the park
with her helmet on.

Then...

S W O O P !

The magpie came flying
out of the trees.
But this time
it didn't swoop at Alex.
It swooped at Dad!

Alex turned around
to see if Dad was hurt.

"The magpie just missed me!"
said Dad.

"I'll have to make **you**
a scary hat, too," said Alex.

16